Quilting with P...

LEISURE ARTS, INC.
Maumelle, Arkansas

EDITORIAL STAFF

Vice President of Editorial: Susan White Sullivan
Creative Art Director: Katherine Laughlin
Publications Director: Leah Lampirez
Special Projects Director: Susan Frantz Wiles
Technical Editor: Lisa Lancaster
Technical Writer: Frances Huddleston
Associate Editor: Jean Lewis
Art Category Manager: Lora Puls
Graphic Artist: Becca Snider Tally
Prepress Technician: Stephanie Johnson
Contributing Photographers: Mark Mathews
Contributing Photo Stylists: Christy Myers

BUSINESS STAFF

President and Chief Executive Officer: Rick Barton
Senior Vice President of Operations: Jim Dittrich
Vice President of Finance: Fred F. Pruss
Vice President of Sales-Retail Books: Martha Adams
Vice President of Mass Market: Bob Bewighouse
Vice President of Technology and Planning:
Laticia Mull Dittrich
Controller: Tiffany P. Childers
Information Technology Director: Brian Roden
Director of E-Commerce: Mark Hawkins
Manager of E-Commerce: Robert Young
Retail Customer Service Manager: Stan Raynor

We have made every effort to ensure that these instructions are accurate and complete. We cannot, however, be responsible for human error, typographical mistakes, or variations in individual work.

Library of Congress Control Number: 2013952258

ISBN-13: 978-1-4647-1263-0

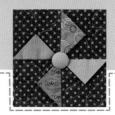

3   Meet Designer Sue Marsh

4   Wild Goose Chase Collection
Throw   4
Table Topper   9
Pillow   12

14   Charming Baby Collection
Quilt   14
Diaper Bag   20

26   Dragons Tooth Quilt

32   Maple Leaf Collection
Table Topper   32
Pillow   38

40   I Love You This Much Quilt

48   Table Charm Collection
Table Runner   48
Placemat   52

55   General Instructions

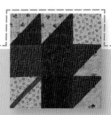

With names like Jelly Roll and Layer Cake, how could a bundle of precut fabrics be anything other than wonderful! They look delicious with their mix of coordinating colors, and their sizes and shapes save you hours of cutting time. The projects in this book show the creative results that are so easy to achieve when you combine a precut collection with yardage of other fabrics. The Wild Goose Chase quilt and other designs demonstrate how the assortments are perfect as focal points, enhanced by borders or blocks of your background fabric. Hooray for precuts!

Meet Designer Sue Marsh

For Sue Marsh of Whistlepig Creek Productions, bags and "smallish quilts" are the kind of projects that drive her passion. "I really enjoy a project that comes together in a short amount of time, as I lose focus quickly. I am always more interested in the next project than the current one."

Sewing from the age of 12, she has loved quick projects since the beginning. "I did my first quilt project from a Quilt in a Day book. I literally made a king-size quilt in a day, and I was hooked."

Sue pursued quilting as a hobby while working in the petroleum industry for 15 years. Then in 1997, she turned to full-time designing of quilt projects and fabrics.

She describes her style as "Random! I like a little bit of everything. My fabric design has been whimsical, with a focus on kids. I've got a couple lines in the works that are modern and good for bag-making."

She still has a soft spot for technology, however.

"I am an engineer by education and a software developer by experience. I love technology and wouldn't/couldn't do my job without software and computerized equipment at my fingertips. The automation takes the tedium out of design and allows me to do the fun stuff."

She especially loves the tools, gadgets, and equipment that are available to quilters. "My house is stuffed with sewing, embroidery, and quilting machines. Plus fabric. Plus thread. Plus patterns. Plus, plus, plus...."

Knowing this about Sue, it's not surprising to hear that her favorite quote is, "If it's worth doing, it's worth doing to excess."

She draws, sews, and quilts at the home she shares with her husband, Bernie, and five cats in a suburb of Denver, Colorado. For more about Sue and Whistlepig Creek Productions, visit her pages on Facebook, Pinterest, and wpcreek.blogspot.com.

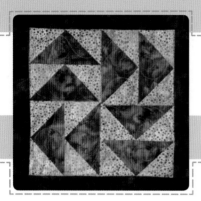

Wild Goose Chase

THROW

Finished Quilt Size:
52" x 61" (132 cm x 155 cm)

Finished Block Size:
8" x 8" (20 cm x 20 cm)

SHOPPING LIST

Yardage is based on 43"/44" (109 cm/112 cm) wide fabric with a usable width of 40" (102 cm). A Jelly Roll includes 40 strips 2¹⁄₂"w (6 cm) x width of fabric.

☐ Jelly Roll **or** 40 strips 2¹⁄₂" (6.4 cm) wide x the width of fabric

☐ ⁵⁄₈ yd (57 cm) of dark purple print fabric for sashings and inner border

☐ 1⁵⁄₈ yds (1.5 m) of light purple print fabric for outer border

☐ 3⁷⁄₈ yds (3.5 m) of fabric for backing

☐ ⁵⁄₈ yd (57 cm) of fabric for binding

You will also need:

☐ 60" x 69" (152 cm x 175 cm) piece of batting

CUTTING THE PIECES

*Follow **Rotary Cutting**, page 55, to cut fabric. Cut all strips from the selvage-to-selvage width of the fabric unless otherwise indicated. Borders are cut longer than needed and will be trimmed to fit quilt top center. All measurements include ¹/₄" seam allowances.*

Divide the 2¹/₂" wide strips into 2 groups of 20, 1 with lighter fabrics and 1 with darker fabrics.

From *each* of 20 light strips:
• Cut 16 **squares** 2¹/₂" x 2¹/₂".

From *each* of 20 dark strips:
• Cut 8 **rectangles** 4¹/₂" x 2¹/₂".

From dark purple print fabric:
• Cut 2 **side inner borders** 1¹/₂" x 50¹/₂", pieced as necessary.
• Cut 2 **top/bottom inner borders** 1¹/₂" x 39¹/₂".
• Cut 4 **horizontal sashings** 1¹/₂" x 35¹/₂".
• Cut 4 strips 1¹/₂" wide. From these strips, cut 15 **vertical sashings** 1¹/₂" x 8¹/₂".

From light purple print fabric:
• Cut 2 *lengthwise* **top/bottom outer borders** 7¹/₂" x 55¹/₂".
• Cut 2 *lengthwise* **side outer borders** 7¹/₂" x 50¹/₂".

From fabric for binding:
• Cut 7 **binding strips** 2¹/₂" wide.

MAKING THE BLOCKS

*Follow **Piecing**, page 56, and **Pressing**, page 57, to make quilt top. Use ¹/₄" seam allowances throughout.*

1. Draw a diagonal line on wrong side of each **square**.
2. For Block, select 16 **squares** from one fabric and 8 **rectangles** from a contrasting fabric.
3. Matching right sides, place 1 square on 1 end of 1 rectangle and stitch along drawn line. Trim ¹/₄" from stitching line *(Fig. 1)*; press open *(Fig. 2)*.

Fig. 1

Fig. 2

4. Place another square on opposite end of rectangle. Stitch and trim as before *(Fig. 3)*. Press open to make **Flying Geese Unit**. Make 8 matching Flying Geese Units.

Fig. 3

Flying Geese Unit (make 8)

5. Sew 2 Flying Geese Units together to make **Unit 1**. Make 4 Unit 1's.

Unit 1 (make 4)

6. Sew 4 Unit 1's together to make **Block**. Block should measure $8^1/2$" x $8^1/2$" including seam allowances.

Block

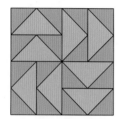

7. Repeat Steps 2-6 to make a total of 20 Blocks.

ASSEMBLING THE QUILT TOP CENTER

1. Sew 4 Blocks and 3 **vertical sashings** together to make **Row**. Row should measure $35^1/2$" x $8^1/2$" including seam allowances. Make 5 Rows.

Row (make 5)

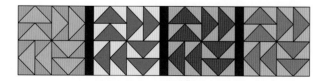

2. Sew 5 Rows and 4 **horizontal sashings** together to make **Quilt Top Center**. Quilt Top Center should measure $35^1/2$" x $44^1/2$" including seam allowances.

ADDING THE BORDERS

1. Follow **Adding Squared Borders**, page 57, to sew **top/bottom** and then **side inner borders** to Quilt Top Center.
2. Sew **side** and then **top/bottom outer borders** to Quilt Top.

COMPLETING THE QUILT

1. Follow **Quilting**, page 58, to mark, layer, and quilt as desired. Quilt shown is machine quilted in the ditch along the outer edges of the blocks and inner border. A swirling pattern is quilted in each block and a feather pattern is quilted in the outer border.
2. Follow **Making a Hanging Sleeve**, page 61, if a hanging sleeve is desired.
3. Use **binding strips** and follow **Binding**, page 61, to make and attach binding.

TABLE TOPPER

Finished Table Topper Size:
26" x 26" (66 cm x 66 cm)

Finished Block Size:
8" x 8" (20 cm x 20 cm)

SHOPPING LIST

Yardage is based on 43"/44" (109 cm/112 cm) wide fabric with a usable width of 40" (102 cm). A Charm Pack includes a variety of 5" x 5" (13 cm x 13 cm) squares.

☐ Charm Pack *or* 32 squares 5" x 5" (13 cm x 13 cm)

☐ ¼ yd (23 cm) of dark brown print fabric for sashings and inner border

☐ ⅜ yd (34 cm) of light brown print fabric for outer border

☐ 1 yd (91 cm) of fabric for backing

☐ ¼ yd (23 cm) of fabric for binding

You will also need:

☐ 34" x 34" (86 cm x 86 cm) piece of batting

CUTTING THE PIECES

*Follow **Rotary Cutting**, page 55, to cut fabric. Cut all strips from the selvage-to-selvage width of the fabric. Borders lengths are exact. All measurements include $^1/_4$" seam allowances.*

Divide the squares into 2 groups of 16, 1 with darker fabrics and 1 with lighter fabrics.

From *each* of 16 dark squares:
• Cut 4 **squares** $2^1/_2$" x $2^1/_2$".

From *each* of 16 light squares:
• Cut 2 **rectangles** $4^1/_2$" x $2^1/_2$".

From dark brown print fabric:
• Cut 2 strips $1^1/_2$" wide. From these strips, cut
  2 **top/bottom inner borders** $1^1/_2$" x $19^1/_2$" and
  2 **side inner borders** $1^1/_2$" x $17^1/_2$".
• Cut 1 strip $1^1/_2$" wide. From this strip, cut
  1 **horizontal sashing** $1^1/_2$" x $17^1/_2$" and
  2 **vertical sashings** $1^1/_2$" x $8^1/_2$".

From light brown print fabric:
• Cut 3 strips $3^1/_2$" wide. From these strips, cut
  2 **top/bottom outer borders** $3^1/_2$" x $25^1/_2$" and
  2 **side outer borders** $3^1/_2$" x $19^1/_2$".

From fabric for binding:
• Cut 3 **binding strips** $2^1/_2$" wide.

MAKING THE BLOCK

*Follow **Piecing**, page 56, and **Pressing**, page 57, to make table topper top. Use $^1/_4$" seam allowances throughout.*

1. Draw a diagonal line on wrong side of each **square**.
2. For Unit 1, select 4 **squares** from one fabric and 2 **rectangles** from a contrasting fabric.
3. Matching right sides, place 1 square on 1 end of 1 rectangle and stitch along drawn line. Trim $^1/_4$" from stitching line *(Fig. 1)*; press open *(Fig. 2)*.

Fig. 1	Fig. 2

4. Place another square on opposite end of rectangle. Stitch and trim as before *(Fig. 3)*. Press open to make **Flying Geese Unit**. Make 2 matching Flying Geese Units.

Fig. 3	Flying Geese Unit (make 2)

5. Sew 2 matching Flying Geese Units together to make **Unit 1**.

Unit 1

6. Repeat Steps 2-5 to make a total of 16 Unit 1's.
7. Sew 4 Unit 1's together to make **Block**. Block should measure 8¹/₂" x 8¹/₂" including seam allowances. Make 4 Blocks.

Block (make 4)

ASSEMBLING THE TABLE TOPPER TOP
Refer to Table Topper Top Diagram to assemble table topper top.
1. Sew 2 Blocks and 1 **vertical sashing** together to make **Row**. Row should measure 17¹/₂" x 8¹/₂" including seam allowances. Make 2 Rows.

Row (make 2)

2. Sew 2 Rows and **horizontal sashing** together to make **Center Section** of Table Topper Top. Center Section should measure 17¹/₂" x 17¹/₂" including seam allowances.

3. Follow **Adding Squared Borders**, page 57, to sew **side** and then **top/bottom inner borders** to Center Section.
4. Sew **outer borders** to Table Topper Top.

COMPLETING THE TABLE TOPPER
1. Follow **Quilting**, page 58, to mark, layer, and quilt as desired. Table Topper shown is machine meander quilted.
2. Use **binding strips** and follow **Binding**, page 61, to make and attach binding.

Table Topper Top Diagram

PILLOW

Finished Pillow Size:
26" x 26" (66 cm x 66 cm) including flange

Finished Block Size:
8" x 8" (20 cm x 20 cm)

SHOPPING LIST

Yardage is based on 43"/44" (109 cm/112 cm) wide fabric with a usable width of 40" (102 cm). A Charm Pack includes a variety of 5" x 5" (13 cm x 13 cm) squares.

☐ Charm Pack *or* 32 squares 5" x 5" (13 cm x 13 cm)

☐ ¼ yd (23 cm) of dark brown print fabric for sashings and inner border

☐ ³⁄₈ yd (34 cm) of light brown print fabric for outer border

☐ ⁷⁄₈ yd (80 cm) of fabric for pillow back

☐ ¼ yd (23 cm) of fabric for binding

You will also need:

☐ 25½" x 25½" (65 cm x 65 cm) piece of fusible fleece

☐ Polyester fiberfill

CUTTING THE PIECES

*Follow **Rotary Cutting**, page 55, to cut fabric. Cut all strips from the selvage-to-selvage width of the fabric. Borders lengths are exact. All measurements include ¹/₄" seam allowances.*

Divide the squares into 2 groups of 16, 1 with darker fabrics and 1 with lighter fabrics.

From *each* of 16 dark squares:
• Cut 4 **squares** 2¹/₂" x 2¹/₂".

From *each* of 16 light squares:
• Cut 2 **rectangles** 4¹/₂" x 2¹/₂".

From dark brown print fabric:
• Cut 2 strips 1¹/₂" wide. From these strips, cut 2 **top/bottom inner borders** 1¹/₂" x 19¹/₂" and 2 **side inner borders** 1¹/₂" x 17¹/₂".
• Cut 1 strip 1¹/₂" wide. From this strip, cut 1 **horizontal sashing** 1¹/₂" x 17¹/₂" and 2 **vertical sashings** 1¹/₂" x 8¹/₂".

From light brown print fabric:
• Cut 3 strips 3¹/₂" wide. From these strips, cut 2 **top/bottom outer borders** 3¹/₂" x 25¹/₂" and 2 **side outer borders** 3¹/₂" x 19¹/₂".

From fabric for pillow back:
• Cut 2 **pillow back pieces** 25¹/₂" x 13".

From fabric for binding:
• Cut 3 **binding strips** 2¹/₂" wide.

MAKING THE PILLOW TOP

1. Follow **Making the Block** and **Assembling the Table Topper Top**, pages 10-11, and refer to **Pillow Top Diagram** to make **Pillow Top**.

COMPLETING THE PILLOW

Match right sides unless otherwise indicated. Use ¹/₄" seam allowances throughout.

1. Follow manufacturer's instructions to fuse fusible fleece to wrong side of Pillow Top. **Note:** *Press on fabric side or use a pressing cloth. Do not place hot iron directly on fleece.*
2. Leaving an opening for stuffing, sew **pillow back pieces** together along one long edge *(**Fig. 1**)* to make pillow back. Open out flat and press seam allowances open.

Fig. 1

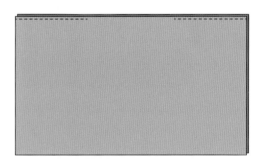

3. With ***wrong*** sides together, layer pillow back and Pillow Top. Quilt in the ditch along inner and outer edges of inner border.
4. Use **binding strips** and follow **Binding**, page 61, to make and attach binding.
5. Stuff pillow with fiberfill; sew opening closed.

Pillow Top Diagram

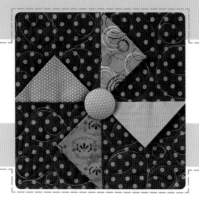

Charming Baby

COLLECTION

QUILT

Finished Quilt Size:
36" x 45" (91 cm x 114 cm)

Finished Block Size:
9" x 9" (23 cm x 23 cm)

SHOPPING LIST

Yardage is based on 43"/44" (109 cm/112 cm) wide fabric with a usable width of 40" (102 cm). A Charm Pack includes a variety of 5" x 5" (13 cm x 13 cm) squares.

- ☐ 2 Charm Packs *or* 48 **squares** 5" x 5" (13 cm x 13 cm)
- ☐ 1 yd (91 cm) of brown/blue polka dot fabric for blocks and outer border
- ☐ ¼ yd (23 cm) of blue print fabric for inner border
- ☐ ⅛ yd (11 cm) *each* of 2 blue print fabrics for covered buttons
- ☐ 3 yds (2.7 m) of fabric for backing
- ☐ ½ yd (46 cm) of fabric for binding

You will also need:

- ☐ 44" x 53" (112 cm x 135 cm) piece of batting
- ☐ Six 2" (51 mm) diameter buttons to cover

CUTTING THE PIECES

*Follow **Rotary Cutting**, page 55, to cut fabric. Cut all strips from the selvage-to-selvage width of the fabric. Borders are cut longer than needed and will be trimmed to fit quilt top center. All measurements include 1/4" seam allowances.*

From brown/blue polka dot fabric:
• Cut 2 **side outer borders** 3 1/2" x the width of the fabric.
• Cut 2 **top/bottom outer borders** 3 1/2" x 39 1/2".
• Cut 3 strips 5" wide. From these strips, cut 24 **background squares** 5" x 5".

From blue print fabric:
• Cut 2 **side inner borders** 1 1/2" x the width of the fabric.
• Cut 2 **top/bottom inner borders** 1 1/2" x 33 1/2".

From fabric for binding:
• Cut 5 **binding strips** 2 1/2" wide.

MAKING THE BLOCKS

*Follow **Piecing**, page 56, and **Pressing**, page 57, to make quilt top. Use 1/4" seam allowances throughout.*

1. Select 24 (6 groups of 4 coordinating) **squares** for pinwheels. Matching wrong sides, press each square in half diagonally *(Fig. 1)*. Press each square again to make **Prairie Point** *(Fig. 2)*.

Fig. 1

Fig. 2

2. Matching raw edges, sew 1 Prairie Point to 1 **background square** to make **Unit 1**. Trim triangle points even with sides of background square to reduce bulk. Make 24 (6 groups of 4 coordinating) Unit 1's.

Unit 1 (make 24)

3. Sew 2 coordinating Unit 1's together to make **Unit 2**. Press seam allowances open. Make 12 Unit 2's.

Unit 2 (make 12)

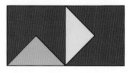

4. Sew 2 coordinating Unit 2's together to make **Pinwheel Block**. Stitch across intersection again to reinforce the center seam. Pick out a couple of stitches in the seam allowances to allow the seam allowances to lie in opposite directions. Block should measure $9^1/2$" x $9^1/2$" including seam allowances. Make 6 Pinwheel Blocks.

Pinwheel Block (make 6)

5. Sew 4 **squares** together to make Four-Patch Block. Block should measure $9^1/2$" x $9^1/2$" including seam allowances. Make 6 Four-Patch Blocks.

Four-Patch Block (make 6)

ASSEMBLING THE QUILT TOP CENTER

*Refer to **Quilt Top Diagram** to assemble quilt top.*

1. Sew 2 Four-Patch Blocks and 1 Pinwheel Block together to make **Row A**. Row should measure $27^1/2$" x $9^1/2$" including seam allowances. Make 2 Row A's.

Row A (make 2)

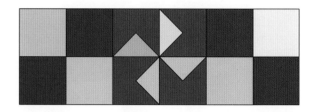

2. Sew 2 Pinwheel Blocks and 1 Four-Patch Block together to make **Row B**. Row should measure $27^1/2$" x $9^1/2$" including seam allowances. Make 2 Row B's.

Row B (make 2)

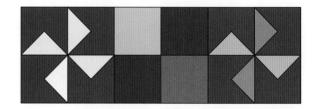

3. Sew Rows together to make **Quilt Top Center**. Center should measure $27^1/2$" x $36^1/2$" including seam allowances.

ADDING THE BORDERS

1. Follow **Adding Squared Borders**, page 57, to sew **side** then **top/bottom inner borders** to Quilt Top Center.
2. In the same manner, sew **outer borders** to Quilt Top.

COMPLETING THE QUILT

1. Follow **Quilting**, page 58, to mark, layer, and quilt as desired. Quilt shown is machine quilted in the ditch along the outer edges of the blocks and inner border. A double-loop pattern is quilted over the entire quilt except for the Prairie Points, which are not quilted or tacked to the quilt.
2. Follow manufacturer's instructions to cover 6 buttons. Sew 1 button to center of each pinwheel.
3. Follow **Making a Hanging Sleeve**, page 61, if a hanging sleeve is desired.
4. Use **binding strips** and follow **Binding**, page 61, to make and attach binding.

Quilt Top Diagram

DIAPER BAG

Finished Bag Size:
13¹/₂" x 13¹/₂" x 4¹/₂" (34 cm x 34 cm x 11 cm)

SHOPPING LIST

Yardage is based on 43"/44" (109 cm/112 cm) wide fabric with a usable width of 40" (102 cm). A Charm Pack includes a variety of 5" x 5" (13 cm x 13 cm) squares. A Fat Quarter is approximately 18" x 22" (46 cm x 56 cm).

☐ Charm Pack *or* 10 squares 5" x 5" (13 cm x 13 cm) for pinwheels and covered buttons (8 cream and 2 blue)

☐ 8 assorted print Fat Quarters (2 brown, 2 blue, and 4 tan)

☐ 1 yd (91 cm) of dark brown for lining

You will also need:

☐ ³/₄ yd (69 cm) of 45" (114 cm) wide fusible fleece

☐ Two 2" (51 mm) buttons to cover

Optional: *For a more rigid bag bottom, you will also need the following to make bottom insert.*

☐ 2 pieces of mat board 13¹/₂" x 4¹/₂" (34 cm x 11 cm), layered and glued together

☐ 2 pieces of fabric 14¹/₄" x 5¹/₄" (36 cm x 13 cm) for **insert covers**

CUTTING THE PIECES

*Follow **Rotary Cutting**, page 55, to cut fabric. Cut strips from yardage from the selvage-to-selvage width of the fabric. Cut strips from fat quarters parallel to the long (22") edge. All measurements include ¹/₄" seam allowances.*

From brown print fat quarter #1:
• Cut 2 strips 5" wide. From these strips, cut 8 **background squares** 5" x 5".

From brown print fat quarter #2:
• Cut 2 strips 5" wide. From these strips, cut 2 **side pockets** 5" x 19".

From blue print fat quarter #1:
• Cut 4 strips 2¹/₂" wide. From these strips, cut 4 **handles** 2¹/₂" x 21".

From blue print fat quarter #2:
• Cut 1 strip 5" wide. From this strip, cut 2 **accent pockets** 5" x 9¹/₂".

From *each* of tan print fat quarter #1 and #2:
• Cut 1 **bag front/back** 14" x 14".

From tan print fat quarter #3:
• Cut 2 strips 5" wide. From these strips, cut 2 **bag sides** 5" x 14".

From tan print fat quarter #4:
• Cut 1 **bag bottom** 5" x 14".

From dark brown print fabric:
• Cut 1 strip 16¹/₄" wide. From this strip, cut 2 **bag linings** 18¹/₂" x 16¹/₄".
• Cut 1 strip 9¹/₂" wide. From this strip, cut 2 **front/back pocket linings** 14" x 9¹/₂".
• Cut 1 strip 6" wide. From this strip, cut 2 **inside pockets** 10" x 6".

From fusible fleece:
• Cut 1 strip 14" wide. From this strip, cut 2 **bag front/backs** 14" x 14".
• Cut 1 strip 2¹/₂" wide. From this strip, cut 2 **handles** 2¹/₂" x 21".
• Cut 1 strip 5" wide. From this strip, cut 2 **bag sides** 5" x 14" and 1 **bag bottom** 5" x 14".

MAKING THE BLOCKS

*Follow **Piecing**, page 56, and **Pressing**, page 57, to make bag. Use ¼" seam allowances throughout.*

1. Using cream **squares** and brown print #1 **background squares**, follow **Making the Blocks**, Steps 1-4, pages 16-18, to make 2 **Pinwheel Blocks**.

Pinwheel Block (make 2)

MAKING THE BAG FRONT AND BACK

1. Sew 1 Pinwheel Block and 1 **accent pocket** together to make **front pocket**. Repeat to make **back pocket**.

Front/Back Pocket (make 2)

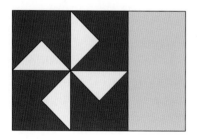

2. Matching right sides, sew 1 **front/back pocket lining** to front pocket along top edge; turn and press. Repeat to sew lining to back pocket.

3. Follow manufacturer's instructions to cover 2 buttons. Sew 1 button to center of each pinwheel.

4. Following manufacturer's instructions, fuse corresponding fleece pieces to **bag front** and **bag back**. Quilt each piece as desired. Bag shown is crosshatch quilted.

5. With right sides facing up and aligning bottom edges, baste front pocket to bag front. Sewing through all layers, topstitch along seam between Block and accent pocket as shown in red (**Fig. 1**). Repeat with back pocket and bag back.

Fig. 1

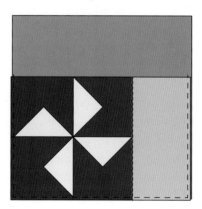

MAKING THE BAG SIDES AND BOTTOM

1. Fuse corresponding fleece pieces to **bag sides** and **bag bottom**. Quilt each piece as desired. Bag shown is crosshatch quilted.
2. Matching short edges and wrong sides, fold each **side pocket** in half; press.
3. Matching raw edges, baste 1 side pocket to right side of each bag side (**Fig. 2**).

Fig. 2

ASSEMBLING THE OUTER BAG

1. Aligning top edges and stopping and backstitching 1/4" from bottom edge of bag side, sew 1 bag side to one side of bag front (**Fig. 3**). Sew remaining bag side to other side of bag front (**Fig. 4**).

Fig. 3

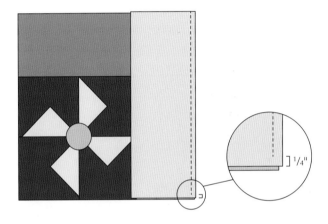

Fig. 4

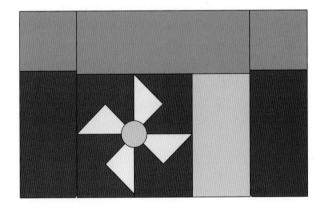

2. In the same manner, sew bag sides to bag back. Do not turn bag right side out.
3. Starting and stopping $1/4$" from corners of bag bottom and backstitching at beginning and end, sew bag bottom to bottom edge of bag *(Fig. 5)*. Turn outer bag right side out.

Fig. 5

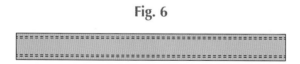

ADDING THE HANDLES
1. Fuse corresponding fleece pieces to 2 **handles**.
2. Matching right sides, sew 1 handle with fleece and 1 handle without fleece together along long edges; turn right side out. Repeat with remaining handles.
3. Topstitch $1/4$" and $3/8$" from long edges of each handle *(Fig. 6)*.

Fig. 6

4. Matching raw edges, baste handles to right sides of bag front and bag back 3" from sides *(Fig. 7)*.

Fig. 7

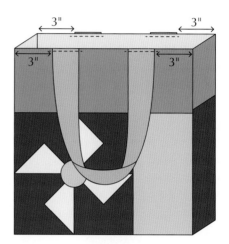

MAKING THE BAG LINING
1. Turning edge under twice, hem 1 long (top) edge of 1 **inside pocket** $1/4$"; topstitch folded edge in place. Press remaining edges $1/4$" to wrong side. With right sides facing up, center and pin pocket $41/2$" from bottom edge of 1 **bag lining**. Sew side and bottom edges of pocket to lining *(Fig. 8)*. Repeat with remaining inside pocket and bag lining.

Fig. 8

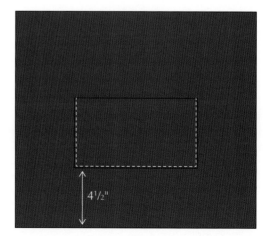

2. Matching right sides and leaving a 6" opening on bottom edge, sew 2 **bag linings** together along side and bottom edges *(Fig. 9)*.

Fig. 9

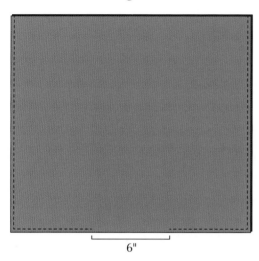

6"

3. To form each bottom corner of bag lining, match 1 side seam to bottom seam. Sew across lining bottom 2¼" from corner point *(Fig. 10)*. Trim seam allowances to ¼". Do not turn bag lining right side out.

Fig. 10

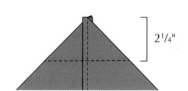

2¼"

COMPLETING THE BAG

1. Matching right sides and top edges, place outer bag inside bag lining with handles sandwiched in between. Sew outer bag and bag lining together along top edge. Turn bag right side out through opening in bag lining. Sew opening closed. Place bag lining inside outer bag.

2. Topstitch ¼" from top edge of bag.

3. To make optional **bottom insert**, sew **insert covers** together leaving 1 short end open. Trim corners and turn right side out. Slip mat board in cover and stitch opening closed. Place bottom insert in bottom of bag.

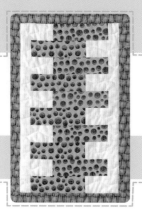

Dragon's Tooth

Finished Quilt Size:
66" x 90" (168 cm x 229 cm)

Finished Block Size:
11" x 17" (28 cm x 43 cm)

SHOPPING LIST

Yardage is based on 43"/44" (109 cm/112 cm) wide fabric with a usable width of 40" (102 cm). A Fat Quarter is approximately 22" x 18" (56 cm x 46 cm).

☐ 16 Fat Quarters* of assorted prints for blocks

☐ 1⁷⁄₈ yds (1.7 m) of pink print fabric for blocks and sashings

☐ 3 yds (2.7 m) of white solid fabric for blocks, sashings, and inner border

☐ 1³⁄₈ yds (1.3 m) of multi-color print fabric for outer border

☐ 5¹⁄₂ yds (5 m) of fabric for backing

☐ ³⁄₄ yd (69 cm) of fabric for binding

You will also need:

☐ 74" x 98" (188 cm x 249 cm) piece of batting

** Fat quarters are required for directional prints. For non-directional prints, a Twice the Charms Roll **or** 16 strips 5¹⁄₂" x 22" (14 cm x 56 cm) may be used instead.*

CUTTING THE PIECES

Follow Rotary Cutting, page 55, to cut fabric. Cut strips from fat quarters parallel to the short edges. Cut strips from Twice the Charm strips parallel to the long edges. Cut all strips from yardage from the selvage-to-selvage width of the fabric. All measurements include ¹/₄" seam allowances.

From *each* fat quarter *or* strip:
• Cut 2 **wide strips** 5¹/₂" x 11".

From pink print fabric:
• Cut 2 strips 15¹/₂" wide. From these strips, cut 32 **side block sashings** 1¹/₂" x 15¹/₂".
• Cut 11 strips 1¹/₂" wide. From these strips, cut 32 **top/bottom block sashings** 11¹/₂" x 1¹/₂".
• Cut 1 strip 3¹/₂" wide. From this strip, cut 9 **sashing squares** 3¹/₂" x 3¹/₂".
• Cut 2 strips 1¹/₂" wide. From these strips, cut 12 **sashing rectangles A** 3¹/₂" x 1¹/₂".
• Cut 1 strip 3¹/₂" wide. From this strip, cut 12 **sashing rectangles B** 1¹/₂" x 3¹/₂".

From white solid fabric:
• Cut 8 **inner border strips** 1¹/₂" wide.
• Cut 11 strips 3¹/₂" wide. From these strips, cut 32 **medium strips** 3¹/₂" x 11".
• Cut 11 strips 1¹/₂" wide. From these strips, cut 32 **narrow strips** 1¹/₂" x 11".
• Cut 10 strips 3¹/₂" wide. From these strips, cut 24 **sashing rectangles C** 3¹/₂" x 8¹/₂" and 24 **sashing rectangles D** 3¹/₂" x 5¹/₂".

From multi-color print fabric:
• Cut 9 **outer border strips** 5¹/₂" wide.

From fabric for binding:
• Cut 9 **binding strips** 2¹/₂" wide.

MAKING THE BLOCKS

Follow Piecing, page 56, and Pressing, page 57, to make quilt top. Use ¹/₄" seam allowances throughout.

1. Sew 1 **medium strip**, 1 **wide strip**, and 1 **narrow strip** together to make **Strip Set A**. Using matching wide strip and making sure direction of print is turned the same as in Strip Set A, sew 1 narrow strip, 1 wide strip, and 1 medium strip together to make **Strip Set B**. Cut along Strip Sets at 2" intervals to make 5 **Unit 1's** and 5 **Unit 2's**.

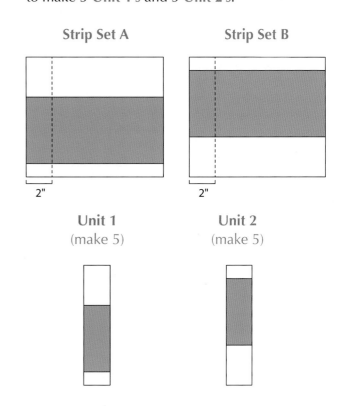

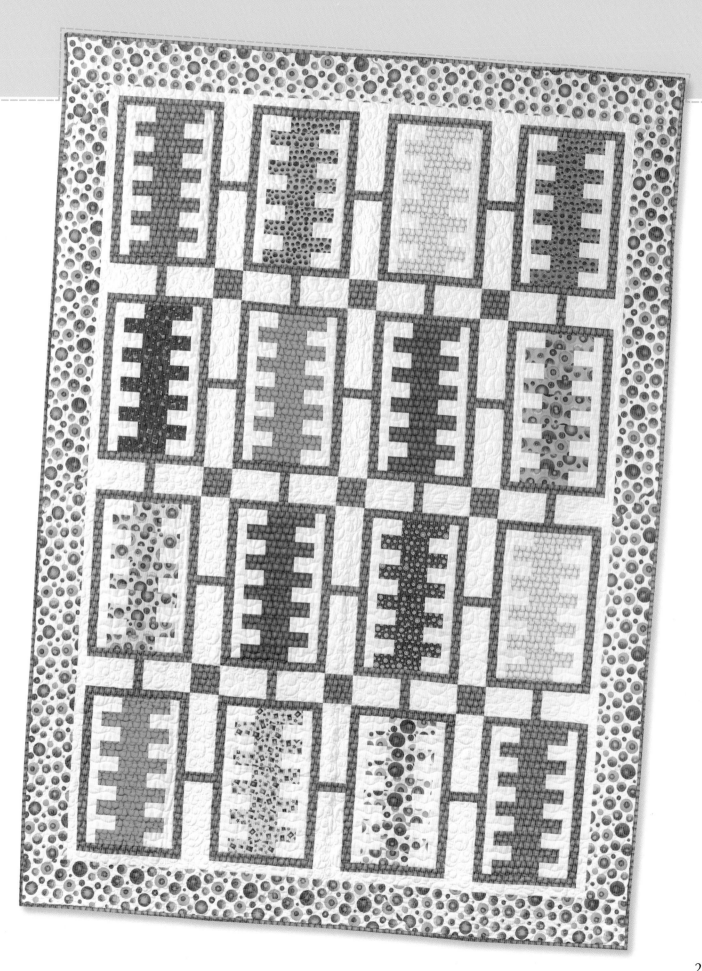

2. Sew 5 Unit 1's and 5 Unit 2's together to make **Unit 3**. Unit 3 should measure $9\frac{1}{2}$" x $15\frac{1}{2}$" including seam allowances.

Unit 3

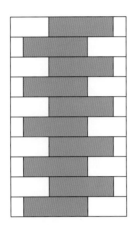

3. Sew **side block sashings** and then **top/bottom block sashings** to Unit 3 to make **Block**. Block should measure $11\frac{1}{2}$" x $17\frac{1}{2}$" including seam allowances.

Block

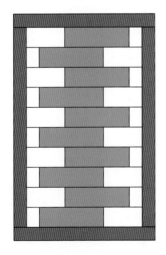

4. Repeat Steps 1-3 to make a total of 16 Blocks.

ASSEMBLING THE QUILT TOP CENTER

Refer to Quilt Top Diagram to assemble quilt top.

1. Sew 1 **sashing rectangle A** and 2 **sashing rectangles C** together to make **vertical sashing**. Make 12 vertical sashings.

Vertical Sashing (make 12)

2. Sew 4 Blocks and 3 vertical sashings together to make **Row**. Row should measure $53\frac{1}{2}$" x $17\frac{1}{2}$" including seam allowances. Make 4 Rows.

Row (make 4)

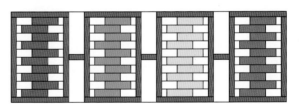

3. Sew 1 **sashing rectangle B** and 2 **sashing rectangles D** together to make **horizontal sashing**. Make 12 horizontal sashings.

Horizontal Sashing (make 12)

4. Sew 4 horizontal sashings and 3 **sashing squares** together to make **Sashing Row**. Sashing Row should measure 53½" x 3½" including seam allowances. Make 3 Sashing Rows.

Sashing Row (make 3)

5. Sew Rows and Sashing Rows together to make **Quilt Top Center**. Quilt Top Center should measure 53½" x 77½" including seam allowances.

ADDING THE BORDERS

1. Sew **inner border strips** together. Follow **Adding Squared Borders**, page 57, to sew **side** and then **top/bottom inner borders** to Quilt Top Center.
2. In the same manner, use **outer border strips** to sew **outer borders** to Quilt Top.

COMPLETING THE QUILT

1. Follow **Quilting**, page 58, to mark, layer, and quilt as desired. Quilt shown is machine quilted, with wavy lines in the blocks and a continuous loop pattern in the sashings and borders.
2. Follow **Making a Hanging Sleeve**, page 61, if a hanging sleeve is desired.
3. Use **binding strips** and follow **Binding**, page 61, to make and attach binding.

Quilt Top Diagram

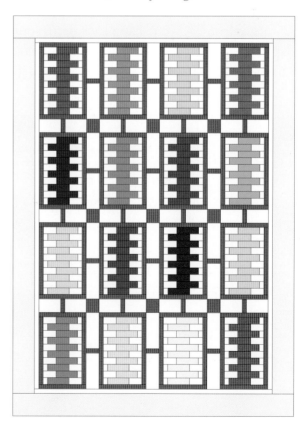

Maple Leaf
COLLECTION

TABLE TOPPER

Finished Table Topper Size:
35¹/₂" x 35¹/₂" (90 cm x 90 cm)

Finished Block Size:
12" x 12" (30 cm x 30 cm)

SHOPPING LIST

Yardage is based on 43"/44" (109 cm/112 cm) wide fabric with a usable width of 40" (102 cm). A Charm Pack includes a variety of 5" x 5" (13 cm x 13 cm) squares.

- ☐ Charm Pack *or* 36 squares 5" x 5" (13 cm x 13 cm) of assorted prints (5 *each* of 4 dark colors for leaves and 16 tan for backgrounds)
- ☐ ⁷/₈ yd (80 cm) of green solid fabric for stems, sashings, and borders
- ☐ ¹/₄ yd (23 cm) of purple solid fabric for sashings and border
- ☐ 1¹/₄ yds (1.1 m) of fabric for backing
- ☐ ³/₈ yd (34 cm) of fabric for binding

You will also need:
- ☐ 44" x 44" (112 cm x 112 cm) piece of batting

CUTTING THE PIECES

*Follow **Rotary Cutting**, page 55, to cut fabric. Cut all strips from the selvage-to-selvage width of the fabric. Borders are cut longer than needed and will be trimmed to fit table topper top center. All measurements include ¼" seam allowances.*

From green solid fabric:
- Cut 2 **top/bottom outer borders** 2" x 39".
- Cut 2 **side outer borders** 2" x 36".
- Cut 2 **top/bottom inner borders** 2" x 35".
- Cut 2 **side inner borders** 2" x 32".
- Cut 4 strips 2" wide. From these strips, cut 4 **wide vertical sashings** 2" x 12½" and 4 **wide horizontal sashings** 2" x 14".
- Cut 1 strip 1" wide. From this strip, cut 4 **stems** 1" x 7".

From purple solid fabric:
- Cut 2 **top/bottom middle borders** 1" x 36".
- Cut 2 **side middle borders** 1" x 35".
- Cut 2 strips 1" wide. From these strips, cut 2 **narrow vertical sashings** 1" x 14" and 1 **narrow horizontal sashing** 1" x 28".

From fabric for binding:
- Cut 4 **binding strips** 2½" wide.

MAKING THE BLOCKS

*Follow **Piecing**, page 56, and **Pressing**, page 57, to make table topper top. Use ¼" seam allowances throughout.*

1. For Block, select 5 **squares** of 1 dark color, 4 tan **squares**, and 1 **stem**.
2. Cut 1 tan square ***once*** diagonally to make 2 triangles. Sew triangles and stem together *(Fig. 1)* to make **Unit 1**. Trim Unit 1 to 4½" x 4½".

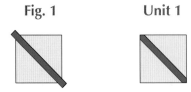

Fig. 1   Unit 1

3. Draw a diagonal line on wrong side of 2 tan **squares**.
4. With right sides together, place 1 marked tan square on top of 1 dark square. Stitch ¼" from each side of drawn line *(Fig. 2)*. Cut along drawn line and press seam allowances to dark fabric to make 2 **Triangle-Squares**. Trim Triangle-Squares to 4½" x 4½". Make 4 Triangle-Squares.

Fig. 2   **Triangle-Square** (make 4)

5. Trim remaining tan square and 3 dark squares to 4½" x 4½".

6. Sew tan square and 2 matching Triangle-Squares together to make **Unit 2**.

Unit 2

7. Sew 1 Triangle-Square and 2 dark squares together to make **Unit 3**.

Unit 3

8. Sew 1 Triangle-Square, 1 dark square, and Unit 1 together to make **Unit 4**.

Unit 4

9. Sew Unit 2, Unit 3, and Unit 4 together to make **Block**. Block should measure 12½" x 12½" including seam allowances.

Block

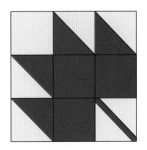

10. Repeat Steps 1-9 to make a total of 4 Blocks.

ASSEMBLING THE TABLE TOPPER TOP CENTER

1. Sew 1 Block, 1 **wide vertical sashing**, and then 1 **wide horizontal sashing** together to make **Unit 5**. Turning Blocks and placing sashings as shown, make **Unit 6**, **Unit 7**, and **Unit 8**.

Unit 5   **Unit 6**

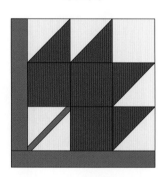

Unit 7   **Unit 8**

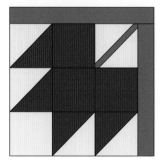
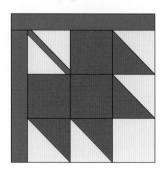

2. Referring to **Table Topper Top Diagram**, sew Unit 5, Unit 6, and 1 **narrow vertical sashing** together to make **Row A**. Row should measure 28" x 14" including seam allowances.

Row A

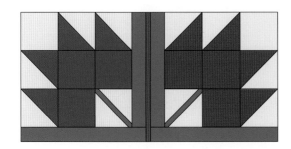

3. Sew Unit 7, Unit 8, and 1 narrow vertical sashing together to make **Row B**. Row should measure 28" x 14" including seam allowances.

Row B

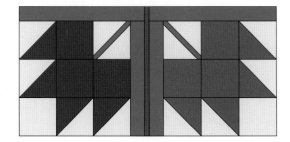

4. Sew Rows and **narrow horizontal sashing** together to make **Center Section** of Table Topper Top. Center Section should measure 28" x 28" including seam allowances.

ADDING THE BORDERS

1. Follow **Adding Squared Borders**, page 57, to sew **side** and then **top/bottom inner borders** to Center Section.
2. In the same manner, sew **middle** and **outer borders** to Table Topper Top.

COMPLETING THE TABLE TOPPER

1. Follow **Quilting**, page 58, to mark, layer, and quilt as desired. Table topper shown is machine meander quilted.
2. Use **binding strips** and follow **Binding**, page 61, to make and attach binding.

Table Topper Top Diagram

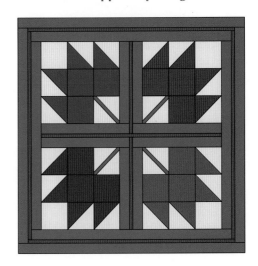

PILLOW

Finished Pillow Size:
17" x 17" (43 cm x 43 cm) including flange

Finished Block Size:
12" x 12" (30 cm x 30 cm)

SHOPPING LIST

Yardage is based on 43"/44" (109 cm/112 cm) wide fabric with a usable width of 40" (102 cm). A Charm Pack includes a variety of 5" x 5" (13 cm x 13 cm) squares.

☐ Charm Pack **or** 9 squares 5" x 5" (13 cm x 13 cm) of assorted prints (5 purple for leaf and 4 tan for background)

☐ ¹/₈ yd (11 cm) of green solid fabric for stem and border

☐ ¹/₄ yd (23 cm) of purple print fabric for borders

☐ ³/₈ yd (34 cm) of fabric for pillow back

You will also need:

☐ 17¹/₂" x 17¹/₂" (44 cm x 44 cm) piece of fusible fleece

☐ Polyester fiberfill

CUTTING THE PIECES

*Follow **Rotary Cutting**, page 55, to cut fabric. Cut all strips from the selvage-to-selvage width of the fabric. Borders lengths are exact. All measurements include ¼" seam allowances.*

From green solid fabric:
- Cut 2 strips 1" wide. From these strips, cut
  2 **top/bottom outer borders** 1" x 15½",
  2 **side middle borders** 1" x 14½", and
  1 **stem** 1" x 7".

From purple print fabric:
- Cut 2 strips 1½" wide. From these strips, cut
  2 **top/bottom outer borders** 1½" x 17½" and
  2 **side outer borders** 1½" x 15½".
- Cut 2 strips 1½" wide. From these strips, cut
  2 **top/bottom inner borders** 1½" x 14½" and
  2 **side inner borders** 1½" x 12½".

From fabric for pillow back:
- Cut 2 **pillow back pieces** 9" x 17½".

MAKING THE PILLOW TOP

*Follow **Piecing**, page 56, and **Pressing**, page 57, to make pillow top. Use ¼" seam allowances throughout.*

1. Follow **Making the Blocks**, Steps 1-9, pages 34-36, to make **Block**.

Block

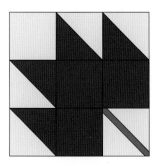

2. Referring to **Pillow Top Diagram** and matching centers and corners, sew **side** and then **top/bottom inner borders** to Block. In the same manner, sew **middle** and **outer borders** to Pillow Top.

Pillow Top Diagram

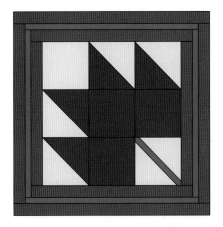

COMPLETING THE PILLOW

Match right sides and use ¼" seam allowances throughout.

1. Follow manufacturer's instructions to fuse fusible fleece to wrong side of Pillow Top. ***Note:*** *Press on fabric side or use a pressing cloth. Do not place hot iron directly on fleece.*
2. Leaving an opening for stuffing, sew **pillow back pieces** together along one long edge (***Fig. 1***) to make pillow back.

Fig. 1

3. Sew Pillow Top and pillow back together. Turn pillow right side out and quilt in the ditch along outer edges of block and borders.
4. Stuff pillow with fiberfill; sew opening closed.

I Love You This Much

Finished Crib Quilt Size:
56⁷/₈" x 56⁷/₈" (144 cm x 144 cm)
Finished Alternate Lap Quilt Size:
71" x 71" (180 cm x 180 cm)

Finished Alternate Twin Quilt Size:
71" x 85¹/₈" (180 cm x 216 cm)
Finished Block Size:
9" x 9" (23 cm x 23 cm)

Note: Instructions are written for the crib size quilt shown in the photo, right, and on page 43, with alternative lap and twin sizes in [ ]. Instructions will be easier to follow if you circle all the numbers pertaining to your desired size quilt. If only one number is given, it applies to all sizes.

SHOPPING LIST

Yardage is based on 43"/44" (109 cm/112 cm) wide fabric with a usable width of 40" (102 cm). A Layer Cake includes a variety of 10" x 10" (25 cm x 25 cm) squares. A Twice the Charm Roll includes a variety of 5¹/₂" x 22" (14 cm x 56 cm) rectangles.

☐ 1 Layer Cake *or* 13 [25, 32] squares 10" x 10" (25 cm x 25 cm) *or* 1 Twice the Charm Roll *or* 13 [25, 32] strips 5¹/₂" x 22" (14 cm x 56 cm)

☐ ¹/₂ yd (46 cm) [1 yd (91 cm), 1¹/₈ yds (1 m)] of white polka dot fabric for blocks

☐ ³/₄ yd (69 cm) [1¹/₄ yds (1.1 m), 1¹/₄ yds (1.1 m)] of white print fabric for setting triangles

☐ ³/₄ yd (69 cm) [1¹/₄ yds (1.1 m), 1³/₈ yds (1.3 m)] of dark purple print fabric for sashings and inner border

☐ 1¹/₈ yds (1 m) [1¹/₄ yds (1.1 m), 1³/₈ yds (1.3 m)] of pink print fabric for outer border

☐ 3⁵/₈ yds (3.3 m) [4¹/₂ yds (4.1 m), 5¹/₄ yds (4.8 m)] of fabric for backing

☐ ⁵/₈ yd (57 cm) [⁵/₈ yd (57 cm), ³/₄ yd (69 cm)] of fabric for binding

You will also need:

☐ 65" x 65" (165 cm x 165 cm) [79" x 79" (201 cm x 201 cm), 79" x 93" (201 cm x 236 cm)] piece of batting

CUTTING THE PIECES

*Follow **Rotary Cutting**, page 55, to cut fabric. Cut all strips from the selvage-to-selvage width of the fabric. All measurements include ¹/₄" seam allowances.*

From *each* of 13 [25, 32] squares or strips:
• Cut 1 **rectangle** 5" x 9¹/₂".
• Cut 1 **large square** 5" x 5".

From white polka dot fabric:
• Cut 2 [4, 4] strips 5" wide. From these strips, cut 13 [25, 32] **large background squares** 5" x 5".
• Cut 3 [5, 7] strips 2" wide. From these strips, cut 52 [100, 128] **small background squares** 2" x 2".

From white print fabric:
• Cut 1 [2, 2] strip(s) 15¹/₂ wide. From this (these) strip(s), cut 2 [3, 4] squares 15¹/₂" x 15¹/₂. Cut squares *twice* diagonally to make 8 [12, 16 (you will use 14)] **side setting triangles**.
• Cut 1 strip 8³/₄" wide. From this strip, cut 2 squares 8³/₄" x 8³/₄". Cut squares *once* diagonally to make 4 **corner setting triangles**.

From dark purple print fabric:
• Cut 16 [25, 30] **sashing and inner border strips** 1¹/₂" wide.

From pink print fabric:
• Cut 6 [7, 8] **outer border strips** 5¹/₂" wide.

From fabric for binding:
• Cut 7 [8, 9] **binding strips** 2¹/₂" wide.

MAKING THE BLOCKS

*Follow **Piecing**, page 56, and **Pressing**, page 57, to make quilt top. Use ¹/₄" seam allowances throughout.*

1. Draw a diagonal line on wrong side of each **small background square**.
2. Matching right sides, place 1 small background square on 2 adjacent corners of 1 **rectangle** and stitch along drawn line; trim ¹/₄" from stitching line *(Fig. 1)*; press open to make **Unit 1**. Make 13 [25, 32] Unit 1's.

Fig. 1   **Unit 1** (make 13 [25, 32])

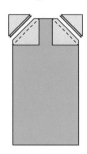 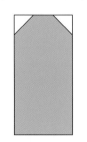

3. In the same manner, sew 2 small background squares to adjacent corners of 1 **large square** to make Unit 2. Make 13 [25, 32] Unit 2's.

Unit 2 (make 13 [25, 32])

4. Sew 1 Unit 2 and 1 **large background square** together to make **Unit 3**. Make 13 [25, 32] Unit 3's.

Unit 3 (make 13 [25, 32])

5. Sew 1 Unit 1 and 1 Unit 3 with matching fabrics together to make **Block**. Block should measure 9^1/$_2$" x 9^1/$_2$" including seam allowances. Make 13 [25, 32] Blocks.

Block (make 13 [25, 32])

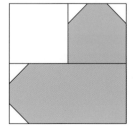

CUTTING THE SASHINGS

1. Using **sashings and inner border strips** and piecing as needed, follow table to cut sashings. Set remainder of strips aside for inner borders.

Cut Length	Number of Sashings		
	Crib	Lap	Twin
81^1/$_2$"	-	-	1
71^1/$_2$"	-	2	2
51^1/$_2$"	2	2	2
31^1/$_2$"	2	2	2
11^1/$_2$"	2	2	2
9^1/$_2$"	18	32	40

Crib Quilt Assembly Diagram

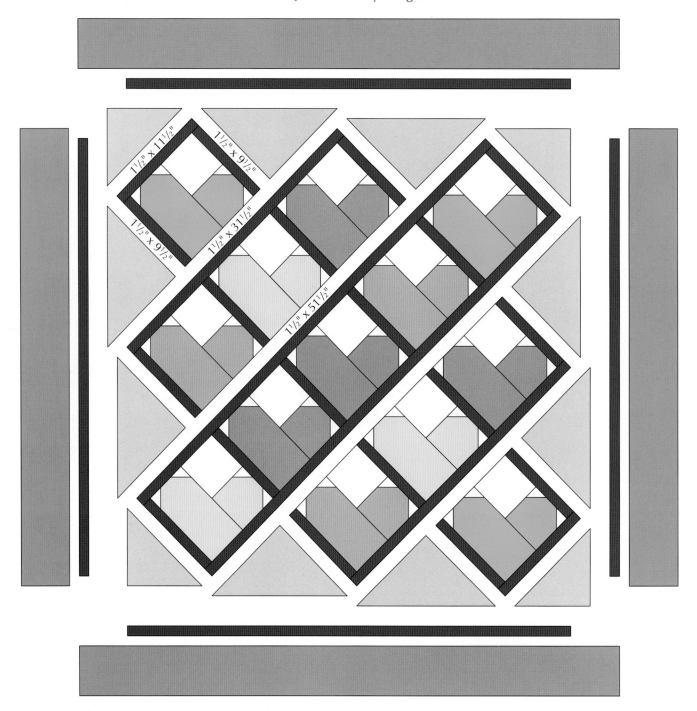

ASSEMBLING THE QUILT TOP CENTER

*Refer to **Assembly Diagram**, page 44 [46, 47], to assemble quilt top. Measurements on diagram indicate cut sizes which include seam allowances.*

1. Sew Blocks, sashings, and **side setting triangles** together to make ***diagonal*** Rows.
2. Sew Rows together and then add **corner setting triangles** to make **Quilt Top Center**. Leaving 1/4" seam allowances beyond corner points of sashings, trim outer edges as needed. Quilt Top Center should measure approximately 44³/₈" x 44³/₈" [58¹/₂" x 58¹/₂", 58¹/₂" x 72⁵/₈"] including seam allowances.

ADDING THE BORDERS

1. Sew strips for inner borders (set aside earlier) together end to end. Follow **Adding Squared Borders**, page 57, to sew **side** and then **top/bottom inner borders** to Quilt Top Center.
2. In the same manner, use **outer border strips** to sew **outer borders** to Quilt Top.

COMPLETING THE QUILT

1. Follow **Quilting**, page 58, to mark, layer, and quilt as desired. Quilt shown is machine quilted. A butterfly motif is quilted in each block and a flower motif is quilted in each setting triangle. A continuous loop pattern is quilted in the sashings and inner border and a continuous flower pattern is quilted in the outer border.
2. Follow **Making a Hanging Sleeve**, page 61, if a hanging sleeve is desired.
3. Use **binding strips** and follow **Binding**, page 61, to make and attach binding.

Crib Quilt Top Diagram

Lap Quilt Assembly Diagram

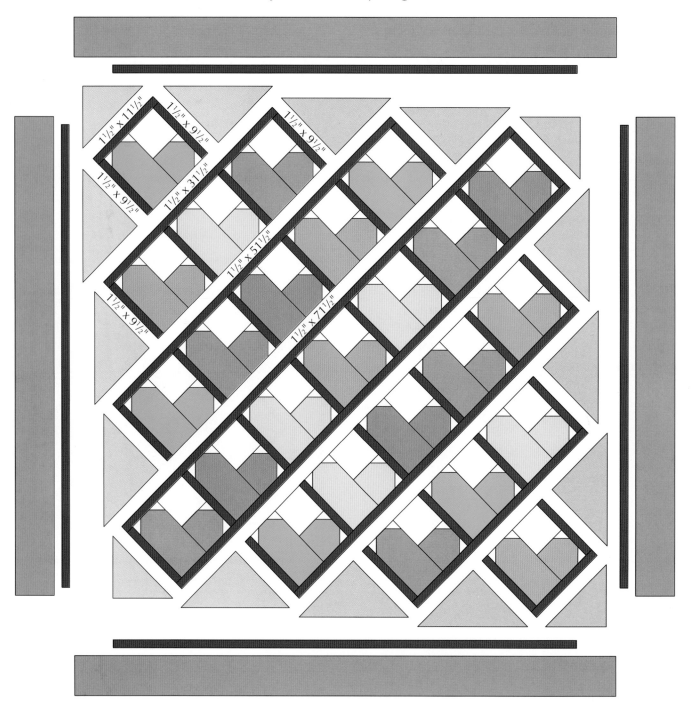

Twin Quilt Assembly Diagram

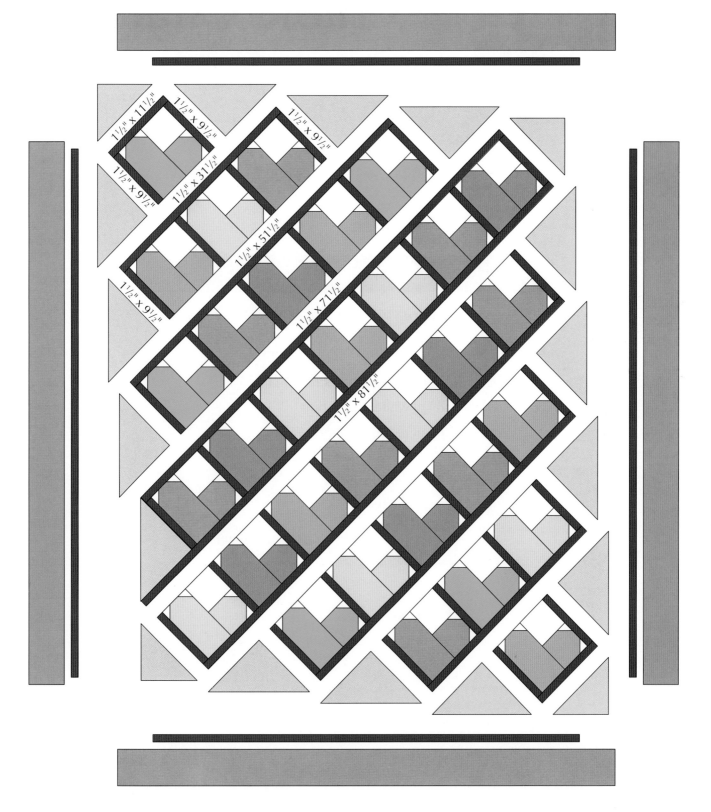

Table Charm

TABLE RUNNER

Finished Table Runner Size:
17¼" x 40⅝" (44 cm x 103 cm)

SHOPPING LIST

Yardage is based on 43"/44" (109 cm/112 cm) wide fabric with a usable width of 40" (102 cm). A Charm Pack includes a variety of 5" x 5" (13 cm x 13 cm) squares.

☐ Charm Pack **or** 27 squares 5" x 5" (13 cm x 13 cm)

☐ ⅜ yd (34 cm) of white solid fabric

☐ ¼ yd (23 cm) of red solid fabric

☐ 1⅜ yds (1.3 m) of fabric for backing

☐ ⅜ yd (34 cm) of fabric for binding

You will also need:

☐ 25¼" x 48⅝" (64 cm x 124 cm) piece of batting

CUTTING THE PIECES

Follow Rotary Cutting, page 55, to cut fabric. Cut all strips from the selvage-to-selvage width of the fabric. All measurements include ¹/₄" seam allowances.

From *each* of 17 squares:
• Cut 4 **squares** 2¹/₂" x 2¹/₂" for a total of 68.

From *each* of 10 squares:
• Cut 2 **rectangles** 2¹/₂" x 5" for a total of 20.

From white solid fabric:
• Cut 4 strips 2¹/₂" wide. From these strips, cut 58 **background squares** 2¹/₂" x 2¹/₂". Cut 2 of these squares *once* diagonally to make 4 **background triangles**.

From red solid fabric:
• Cut 4 **sashings** 1" x 40¹/₂", pieced as needed.

From fabric for binding:
• Cut 4 **binding strips** 2¹/₂" wide.

MAKING THE TABLE RUNNER TOP

Follow Piecing, page 56, and Pressing, page 57, to make table runner top. Use ¹/₄" seam allowances throughout.

1. Sew 1 **square** and 2 **background squares** together to make **Unit 1**. Make 28 Unit 1's.

Unit 1 (make 28)

2. Off-setting units as shown in **Fig. 1**, sew 14 Unit 1's and 2 **background triangles** together. Leaving ¹/₄" seam allowances beyond corner points of squares, trim edges to make **Unit 2**. Make 2 Unit 2's.

Fig. 1

Unit 2 (make 2)

3. Measure length across the center of each Unit 2. If measurements are not the same, make seams between Unit 1's slightly larger or smaller as needed. Trim 4 **sashings** to same length as Unit 2's. Sew 2 sashings and 1 Unit 2 together to make **Diamond Panel**. Make 2 Diamond Panels.

Diamond Panel (make 2)

4. Sew 20 **rectangles** together to make **Unit 3**.

Unit 3

5. Sew 20 **squares** together to make **Unit 4**. Make 2 Unit 4's.

Unit 4 (make 2)

6. Measure length of each Diamond Panel, Unit 3, and Unit 4. If measurements are not the same, make seams in Unit 3 and Unit 4's slightly larger or smaller as needed.
7. Sew Diamond Panels, Unit 3, and Unit 4's together to make **Table Runner Top**.

COMPLETING THE TABLE RUNNER
1. Follow **Quilting**, page 58, to mark, layer, and quilt as desired. Table Runner shown is machine quilted with a continuous loop pattern.
2. Use **binding strips** and follow **Binding**, page 61, to make and attach binding.

PLACEMAT

Finished Placemat Size:
20⁷/₈" x 15¹/₄" (53 cm x 39 cm)

SHOPPING LIST

Yardage listed is for 2 placemats. Yardage is based on 43"/44" (109 cm/112 cm) wide fabric with a usable width of 40" (102 cm). A Charm Pack includes a variety of 5" x 5" (13 cm x 13 cm) squares.

☐ Charm Pack *or* 22 squares 5" x 5" (13 cm x 13 cm)

☐ ³/₈ yd (34 cm) of white solid fabric

☐ ¹/₄ yd (23 cm) of red solid fabric

☐ 1³/₈ yds (1.3 m) of fabric for backing

☐ ¹/₂ yd (46 cm) of fabric for binding

You will also need:

☐ Two 29" x 23" (74 cm x 58 cm) pieces of batting

CUTTING THE PIECES

*Follow **Rotary Cutting**, page 55, to cut fabric. Cut all strips from the selvage-to-selvage width of the fabric. All measurements include ¹/₄" seam allowances.*

From *each* of 12 squares:
• Cut 4 **squares** 2¹/₂" x 2¹/₂" for a total of 48.

From *each* of 10 squares:
• Cut 2 **rectangles** 2¹/₂" x 5" for a total of 20.

From white solid fabric:
• Cut 4 strips 2¹/₂" wide. From these strips, cut 60 **background squares** 2¹/₂" x 2¹/₂". Cut 4 of these squares *once* diagonally to make 8 **background triangles**.

From red solid fabric:
• Cut 8 **sashings** 1" x 20¹/₂".

From fabric for binding:
• Cut 5 **binding strips** 2¹/₂" wide.

MAKING THE PLACEMAT TOPS

*Follow **Piecing** page 56, and **Pressing**, page 57, to make placemat tops. Use ¹/₄" seam allowances throughout.*

1. Sew 1 **square** and 2 **background squares** together to make **Unit 1**. Make 28 Unit 1's.

Unit 1 (make 28)

2. Off-setting units as shown in **Fig. 1**, sew 7 Unit 1's and 2 **background triangles** together. Leaving ¹/₄" seam allowances beyond corner points of squares, trim edges to make **Unit 2**. Make 4 Unit 2's.

Fig. 1

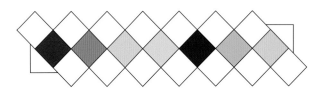

Unit 2 (make 4)

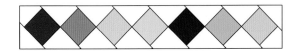

3. Measure length across the center of each Unit 2. If measurements are not the same, make seams between Unit 1's slightly larger or smaller as needed. Trim 8 **sashings** to same length as Unit 2's. Sew 2 sashings and 1 Unit 2 together to make **Diamond Panel**. Make 4 Diamond Panels.

Diamond Panel (make 4)

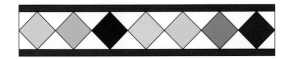

4. Sew 10 **rectangles** together to make **Unit 3**. Make 2 Unit 3's.

Unit 3 (make 2)

7. Sew 2 Diamond Panels, 1 Unit 3, and 1 Unit 4 together to make **Placemat Top**. Make 2 Placemat Tops.

COMPLETING THE PLACEMATS

1. Follow **Quilting**, page 58, to mark, layer, and quilt as desired. Placemats shown are machine quilted with a continuous loop pattern.

2. Use **binding strips** and follow **Binding**, page 61, to make and attach binding.

5. Sew 10 **squares** together to make **Unit 4**. Make 2 Unit 4's.

Unit 4 (make 2)

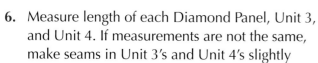

6. Measure length of each Diamond Panel, Unit 3, and Unit 4. If measurements are not the same, make seams in Unit 3's and Unit 4's slightly larger or smaller as needed.

Shown here is the Table Charm Collection made with yellow, green, orange, and blue florals. Notice that rectangles were used in place of the squares along the outer edges.

General Instructions

To make your quilting easier and more enjoyable, we encourage you to carefully read all of the general instructions, study the color photographs, and familiarize yourself with the individual project instructions before beginning a project.

FABRICS
SELECTING FABRICS
Choose high-quality, medium-weight 100% cotton fabrics. All-cotton fabrics hold a crease better, fray less, and are easier to quilt than cotton/polyester blends.

Yardage requirements listed for each project are based on 43"/44" wide fabric with a "usable" width of 40" after shrinkage and trimming selvages. Actual usable width will probably vary slightly from fabric to fabric. Our recommended yardage lengths should be adequate for occasional re-squaring of fabric when many cuts are required.

PREPARING FABRICS
Pre-washing fabrics may cause edges to ravel. As a result, your pre-cut fabric pieces may not be large enough to cut all of the pieces required for your chosen project. Therefore, we do not recommend pre-washing your yardage or pre-cut fabrics.

Before cutting, prepare fabrics with a steam iron set on cotton and starch or sizing. The starch or sizing will give the fabric a crisp finish. This will make cutting more accurate and may make piecing easier.

ROTARY CUTTING
CUTTING FROM YARDAGE
- Place fabric on work surface with fold closest to you.

- Cut all strips from the selvage-to-selvage width of the fabric unless otherwise indicated in project instructions.

- Square left edge of fabric using rotary cutter and rulers *(Figs. 1-2)*.

Fig. 1

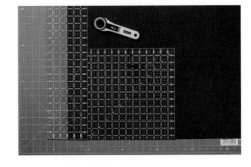

Fig. 2

- To cut each strip required for a project, place ruler over cut edge of fabric, aligning desired marking on ruler with cut edge; make cut *(Fig. 3)*.

Fig. 3

- When cutting several strips from a single piece of fabric, it is important to make sure that cuts remain at a perfect right angle to the fold; square fabric as needed.

CUTTING FROM PRECUTS

- Place fabric flat on work surface with short edge closest to you.

- Unless otherwise instructed, cut all strips parallel to the long edge of the fabric in the same manner as cutting from yardage.

- To cut each strip required for a project, place ruler over cut edge of fabric, aligning desired marking on ruler with cut edge; make cut.

PIECING
Precise cutting, followed by accurate piecing, will ensure that all pieces will fit together well.

- Set sewing machine stitch length for approximately 11 stitches per inch.

- Use neutral-colored general-purpose sewing thread (not quilting thread) in needle and in bobbin.

- An accurate $1/4$" seam allowance is *essential*. Presser feet that are $1/4$" wide are available for most sewing machines.

- When piecing, always place pieces right sides together and match raw edges; pin if necessary.

- Chain piecing saves time and will usually result in more accurate piecing.

- Trim away points of seam allowances that extend beyond edges of sewn pieces.

SEWING ACROSS SEAM INTERSECTIONS
When sewing across the intersection of two seams, place pieces right sides together and match seams exactly, making sure seam allowances are pressed in opposite directions *(Fig. 4)*.

Fig. 4

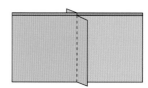

SEWING SHARP POINTS

To ensure sharp points when joining triangular or diagonal pieces, stitch across the center of the "X" (shown in pink) formed on wrong side by previous seams *(Fig. 5)*.

Fig. 5

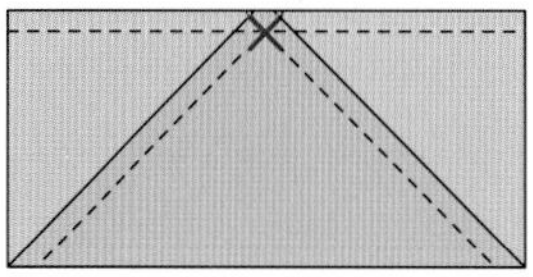

PRESSING

- Use steam iron set on "Cotton" for all pressing.

- Press after sewing each seam.

- Seam allowances are almost always pressed to one side, usually toward the darker fabric. However, to reduce bulk it may occasionally be necessary to press seam allowances toward the lighter fabric or even to press them open.

- To prevent dark fabric seam allowance from showing through light fabric, trim darker seam allowance slightly narrower than lighter seam allowance.

- To press long seams, such as those in long strip sets, without curving or other distortion, lay strips across width of the ironing board.

- When sewing blocks into rows, seam allowances may be pressed in one direction in odd numbered rows and in the opposite direction in even numbered rows. When sewing rows together, press seam allowances in one direction.

ADDING SQUARED BORDERS

1. Mark the center of each edge of quilt top.
2. In most cases, the borders are added to sides, then top and bottom edges of a quilt top. To determine length of side borders, measure **length** across center of quilt top *(Fig. 6)*. Cut 2 side borders from continuous strip *or* trim side borders the determined length.

Fig. 6

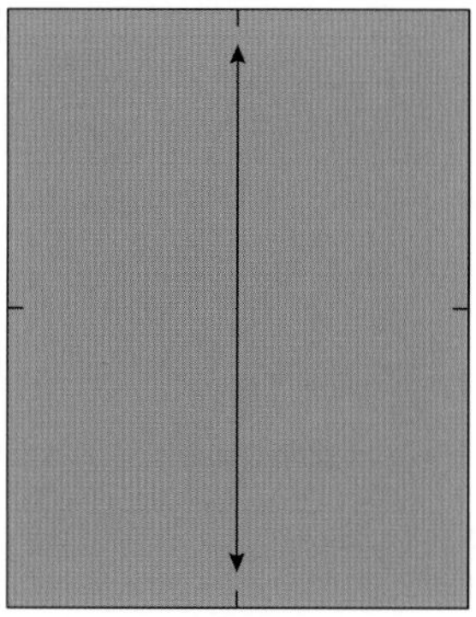

3. Mark the center of 1 long edge of 1 side border. Matching center marks and raw edges, pin border to quilt top, easing in any fullness; stitch. In the same manner, add remaining side border to quilt top.
4. To determine length of top/bottom borders, measure the **width** across center of quilt top (including added borders). Cut 2 top/bottom borders from continuous strip *or* trim top/bottom borders the determined length. Repeat Step 3 to add the top/bottom borders to the quilt top *(Fig. 7)*.

Fig. 7

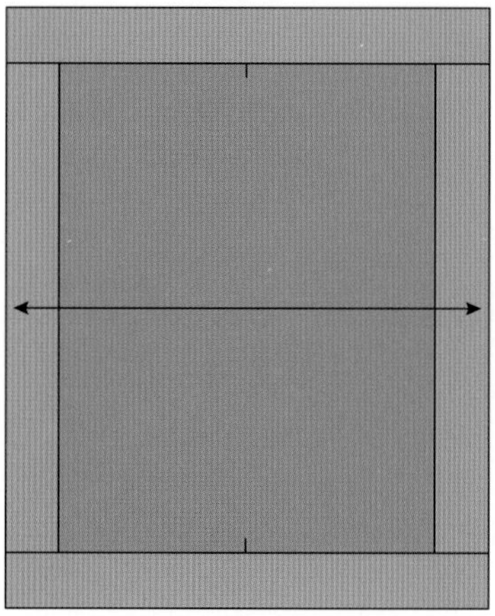

QUILTING

Quilting holds the three layers (top, batting, and backing) of the quilt together and can be done by hand or machine. Because marking, layering, and quilting are interrelated and may be done in different orders depending on circumstances, please read the entire **Quilting** *section, pages 58-60, before beginning project.*

TYPES OF QUILTING DESIGNS

In the Ditch Quilting
Quilting along seamlines or along edges of appliquéd pieces is called "in the ditch" quilting. This type of quilting should be done on the side **opposite** the seam allowance and does not have to be marked.

Outline Quilting
Quilting a consistent distance, usually ¼", from seam or appliqué is called "outline" quilting. Outline quilting may be marked, or ¼" masking tape may be placed along seamlines for quilting guide. (Do not leave tape on quilt longer than necessary, since it may leave an adhesive residue.)

Motif Quilting
Quilting a design, such as a feathered wreath, is called "motif" quilting. This type of quilting should be marked before basting quilt layers together.

Echo Quilting
Quilting that follows the outline of an appliquéd or pieced design with two or more parallel lines is called "echo" quilting. This type of quilting does not need to be marked.

Channel Quilting
Quilting with straight, parallel lines is called "channel" quilting. This type of quilting may be marked or stitched using a guide.

Crosshatch Quilting
Quilting straight lines in a grid pattern is called "crosshatch" quilting. Lines may be stitched parallel to edges of quilt or stitched diagonally. This type of quilting may be marked or stitched using a guide.

Meandering Quilting
Quilting in random curved lines and swirls is called "meandering" quilting. Quilting lines should not cross or touch each other. This type of quilting does not need to be marked.

Stipple Quilting
Meandering quilting that is very closely spaced is called "stipple" quilting. Stippling will flatten the area quilted and is often stitched in background areas to raise appliquéd or pieced designs. This type of quilting does not need to be marked.

MARKING QUILTING LINES
Quilting lines may be marked using fabric marking pencils, chalk markers, or water- or air-soluble pens.

Simple quilting designs may be marked with chalk or chalk pencil after basting. A small area may be marked, then quilted, before moving to next area to be marked. Intricate designs should be marked before basting using a more durable marker.

Caution: Pressing may permanently set some marks. **Test** different markers **on scrap fabric** to find one that marks clearly and can be thoroughly removed.

A wide variety of pre-cut quilting stencils, as well as entire books of quilting patterns, are available. Using a stencil makes it easier to mark intricate or repetitive designs.

To make a stencil from a pattern, center template plastic over pattern and use a permanent marker to trace pattern onto plastic. Use a craft knife with single or double blade to cut channels along traced lines *(Fig. 8)*.

Fig. 8

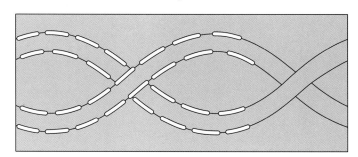

PREPARING THE BACKING

To allow for slight shifting of quilt top during quilting, backing should be approximately 4" larger on all sides. Yardage requirements listed for quilt backings are calculated for 43"/44" wide fabric. To piece a backing, use the following instructions.

1. Measure length and width of quilt top; add 8" to each measurement.
2. Cut backing fabric into two lengths slightly longer than determined *length* measurement. Trim selvages. Place lengths with right sides facing and sew long edges together, forming tube *(Fig. 9)*. Match seams and press along one fold *(Fig. 10)*. Cut along pressed fold to form single piece *(Fig. 11)*.

Fig. 9   Fig. 10

Fig. 11

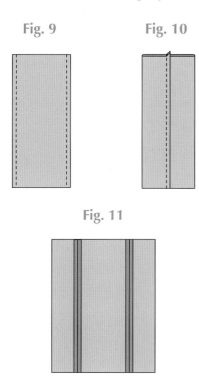

3. Trim backing to size determined in Step 1; press seam allowances open.

CHOOSING THE BATTING

The appropriate batting will make quilting easier. For fine hand quilting, choose low-loft batting. All cotton or cotton/polyester blend battings work well for machine quilting because the cotton helps "grip" quilt layers. If quilt is to be tied, a high-loft batting, sometimes called extra-loft or fat batting, may be used to make quilt "fluffy."

Types of batting include cotton, polyester, wool, cotton/polyester blend, cotton/wool blend, and silk.

When selecting batting, refer to package labels for characteristics and care instructions. Cut batting same size as prepared backing.

ASSEMBLING THE QUILT

1. Examine the wrong side of the quilt top closely; trim any seam allowances and clip any threads that may show through the front of the quilt. Press quilt top, being careful not to "set" any marked quilting lines.
2. Place backing **wrong** side up on flat surface. Use masking tape to tape edges of backing to surface. Place batting on top of backing fabric. Smooth batting gently, being careful not to stretch or tear. Center quilt top **right** side up on batting.
3. Use 1" rustproof safety pins to "pin-baste" all layers together, spacing pins approximately 4" apart. Begin at center and work toward outer edges to secure all layers. If possible, place pins away from areas that will be quilted, although pins may be removed as needed when quilting.

MACHINE QUILTING METHODS

Use general-purpose thread in the bobbin. Do not use quilting thread. Thread the needle of machine with general-purpose thread or transparent monofilament thread to make quilting blend with quilt top fabrics. Use decorative thread, such as a metallic or contrasting-color general-purpose thread, to make quilting lines stand out more.

Straight-Line Quilting

The term "straight-line" is somewhat deceptive, since curves (especially gentle ones) as well as straight lines can be stitched with this technique.

1. Set stitch length for six to ten stitches per inch and attach walking foot to sewing machine.
2. Determine which section of the quilt will have longest continuous quilting line, oftentimes the area from center top to center bottom. Roll up and secure each edge of quilt to help reduce the bulk, keeping fabrics smooth. Smaller projects may not need to be rolled.
3. Begin stitching on the longest quilting line, using very short stitches for the first 1/4" to "lock" quilting. Stitch across project, using one hand on each side of walking foot to slightly spread fabric and to guide fabric through machine. Lock stitches at end of quilting line.
4. Continue machine quilting, stitching longer quilting lines first to stabilize quilt before moving on to other areas.

Free-Motion Quilting

Free-motion quilting may be free form or may follow a marked pattern.

1. Attach a darning foot to the sewing machine and lower or cover feed dogs.
2. Position quilt under darning foot; lower foot. Holding the top thread, take a stitch and pull bobbin thread to top of quilt. To "lock" beginning of quilting line, hold top and bobbin threads while making three to five stitches in place.
3. Use one hand on each side of darning foot to slightly spread fabric and to move fabric through the machine. Even stitch length is achieved by using smooth, flowing hand motion and steady machine speed. Slow machine speed and fast hand movement will create long stitches. Fast machine speed and slow hand movement will create short stitches. Move quilt sideways, back and forth, in a circular motion, or in a random motion to create desired designs; do not rotate quilt. Lock stitches at the end of each quilting line.

MAKING A HANGING SLEEVE

Attaching a hanging sleeve to the back of a quilt before the binding is added allows your project to be displayed on a wall.

1. Measure the width of quilt top edge and subtract 1". Cut a piece of fabric 7" wide by determined measurement.
2. Press short edges of fabric piece 1/4" to wrong side; press edges 1/4" to wrong side again and machine stitch in place.
3. Matching wrong sides, fold piece in half lengthwise to form a tube.
4. **For hand-finished binding:** Follow project instructions to sew binding to quilt top. Before Blindstitching binding to backing, match raw edges and stitch hanging sleeve to center top edge on back of quilt.

   For machine-finished binding: Follow project instructions to zigzag quilt edges and trim batting and backing. Before sewing binding to quilt, match raw edges and sew hanging sleeve to center top edge on back of quilt.
5. Finish binding quilt, treating hanging sleeve as part of backing.
6. Blindstitch bottom of hanging sleeve to backing, taking care not to stitch through to front of quilt.
7. Insert dowel or slat into hanging sleeve.

BINDING
MAKING BINDING

1. Using diagonal seams *(Fig. 12)*, sew strips for binding called for in project together to make one continuous strip.

Fig. 12

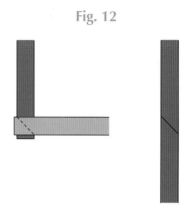

2. Matching wrong sides and raw edges, carefully press continuous strips in half lengthwise to complete binding.

ATTACHING HAND-FINISHED BINDING

1. Beginning with one end near center on bottom edge of quilt, lay binding around quilt to make sure that seams in binding will not end up at a corner. Adjust placement if necessary. Matching raw edges of binding to raw edge of quilt top, pin binding to right side of quilt along one edge.
2. When you reach first corner, mark 1/4" from corner of quilt top *(Fig. 13)*.

Fig. 13

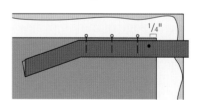

3. Beginning approximately 10" from end of binding and using ¼" seam allowance, sew binding to quilt, backstitching at beginning of stitching and at mark *(Fig. 14)*. Lift needle out of fabric and clip thread.

Fig. 14

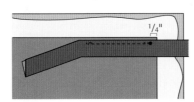

4. Fold binding as shown in *Figs. 15-16* and pin binding to adjacent side, matching raw edges. When you've reached the next corner, mark ¼" from edge of quilt top.

Fig. 15

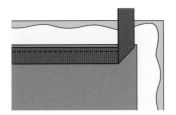

Fig. 16

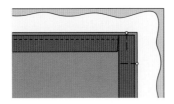

5. Backstitching at edge of quilt top, sew pinned binding to quilt *(Fig. 17)*; backstitch at the next mark. Lift needle out of fabric and clip thread.

Fig. 17

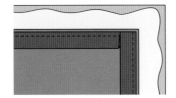

6. Continue sewing binding to quilt, stopping approximately 10" from starting point *(Fig. 18)*.

Fig. 18

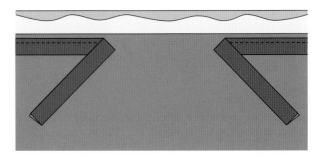

7. Bring beginning and end of binding to center of opening and fold each end back, leaving a ¼" space between folds *(Fig. 19)*. Finger press folds.

Fig. 19

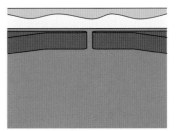

8. Unfold ends of binding and draw a line across wrong side in finger-pressed crease. Draw a line through the lengthwise pressed fold of binding at the same spot to create a cross mark. With edge of ruler at cross mark, line up 45° angle marking on ruler with one long side of binding. Draw a diagonal line from edge to edge. Repeat on remaining end, making sure that the two diagonal lines are angled the same way *(Fig. 20)*.

Fig. 20

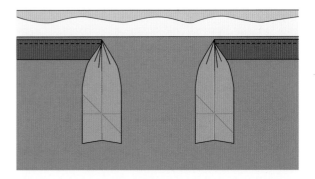

9. Matching right sides and diagonal lines, pin binding ends together at right angles *(Fig. 21)*.

Fig. 21

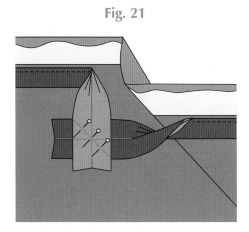

10. Machine stitch along diagonal line *(Fig. 22)*, removing pins as you stitch.

Fig. 22

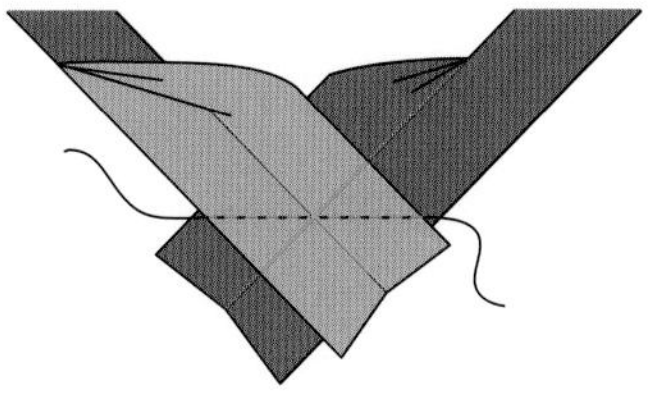

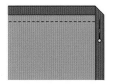

11. Lay binding against quilt to double check that it is correct length.
12. Trim binding ends, leaving ¼" seam allowance; press seam open. Stitch binding to quilt.

13. Trim backing and batting a scant ¼" larger than quilt top so that batting and backing will fill the binding when it is folded over to quilt backing.
14. On one edge of quilt, fold binding over to quilt backing and pin pressed edge in place, covering stitching line *(Fig. 23)*. On adjacent side, fold binding over, forming a mitered corner *(Fig. 24)*. Repeat to pin remainder of binding in place.

Fig. 23

Fig. 24

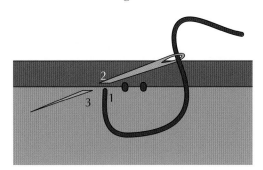

15. Blindstitch binding to backing, taking care not to stitch through to front of quilt. To Blindstitch, come up at 1, go down at 2, and come up at 3 *(Fig. 25)*.

Fig. 25

ATTACHING MACHINE-FINISHED BINDING

For a quick and easy finish when attaching binding, sew binding to the back of the quilt and machine topstitch it in place on the front, eliminating all hand stitching.

1. Using a narrow zigzag, stitch around quilt top close to raw edges *(Fig. 26)*. Trim backing and batting a scant ¼" larger than quilt top.

Fig. 26

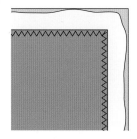

2. Beginning with one end near center on bottom edge of quilt, lay binding around quilt to make sure that seams in binding will not end up at a corner. Adjust placement if necessary. Matching raw edges of binding to raw edge of quilt, pin binding to the backing side of quilt along one edge.

3. Follow Steps 2-12 of **Attaching Hand-Finished Binding**, page 61, folding binding over to quilt front. Machine topstitch binding close to pressed edge *(Fig. 27)*.

Fig. 27

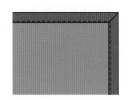

SIGNING AND DATING YOUR QUILT

A completed quilt is a work of art and should be signed and dated. There are many different ways to do this and numerous books on the subject. The label should reflect the style of the quilt, the occasion or person for which it was made, and the quilter's own particular talents. Following are suggestions for recording the history of quilt or adding a sentiment for future generations.

- Embroider quilter's name, date, and any additional information on quilt top or backing. Matching floss, such as cream floss on white border, will leave a subtle record. Bright or contrasting floss will make the information stand out.

- Make label from muslin and use permanent marker to write information. Use different colored permanent markers to make label more decorative. Stitch label to back of quilt.

- Use photo-transfer paper to add image to white or cream fabric label. Stitch label to back of quilt.

- Piece an extra block from quilt top pattern to use as label. Add information with permanent fabric pen. Appliqué block to back of quilt.

Metric Conversion Chart	
Inches x 2.54 = centimeters (cm)	Yards x .9144 = meters (m)
Inches x 25.4 = millimeters (mm)	Yards x 91.44 = centimeters (cm)
Inches x .0254 = meters (m)	Centimeters x .3937 = inches (")
	Meters x 1.0936 = yards (yd)

Standard Equivalents					
⅛"	3.2 mm	0.32 cm	⅛ yard	11.43 cm	0.11 m
¼"	6.35 mm	0.635 cm	¼ yard	22.86 cm	0.23 m
⅜"	9.5 mm	0.95 cm	⅜ yard	34.29 cm	0.34 m
½"	12.7 mm	1.27 cm	½ yard	45.72 cm	0.46 m
⅝"	15.9 mm	1.59 cm	⅝ yard	57.15 cm	0.57 m
¾"	19.1 mm	1.91 cm	¾ yard	68.58 cm	0.69 m
⅞"	22.2 mm	2.22 cm	⅞ yard	80 cm	0.8 m
1 "	25.4 mm	2.54 cm	1 yard	91.44 cm	0.91 m